John Fitzgerald Kennedy:
AMERICA'S
35TH PRESIDENT

John Fitzgerald Kennedy:
AMERICA'S 35TH PRESIDENT

Barry Denenberg

SCHOLASTIC INC.
New York Toronto London Auckland Sydney

PHOTO CREDITS

Cover, Manfred Kreiner/Black Star; pp. viii, 2, 6, 8, 12, 16, 21, 24, 31, 34, 39, 42, 77, 80, 88, 92, John F. Kennedy Library; p. 27, Pictorial Parade; pp. 28, 52, 56, 100, 102, AP/Wide World; pp. 48, 61(top), 61(bottom), 67, 70, 73, 82, 86, 95, United Press; p. 103, UPI/Bettmann Newsphotos.

ISBN 0-590-41344-9

Copyright © 1988 by Barry Denenberg. All rights reserved. Published by Scholastic Inc.

12 11 10 9 8 7 6 5 4 3 2   9/8 0 1 2 3/9

Printed in the U.S.A.   11

First Scholastic printing, November 1988

Contents

A Thousand Days

On a cold and cloudless day in January 1961, John Fitzgerald Kennedy was inaugurated as the thirty-fifth President of the United States. At forty-four he was the youngest man to be elected President in the history of the country. He was also the first one born in the twentieth century. His wife Jacqueline was thirty-two, his daughter Caroline four, and John Jr. was only two months old.

A youthful feeling embraced the thousands lining Pennsylvania Avenue for the inaugural parade and the millions more watching at home on television. Americans across the country shared a sense that they were participating in a momentous event. People felt good. Optimism was in fashion.

But John Kennedy was to serve only three years, a thousand days as it came to be called.

On November 22, 1963, as once again millions watched at home on their television sets, President Kennedy was killed by a twenty-four-year-old assassin while riding in a motorcade through the streets of Dallas, Texas.

In a moment the promise was over. The optimism no more. The story had ended.

It is said that the journey, not the arrival, is what matters. The journey that took John Kennedy from boyhood to the highest office in the land was filled with deep sadness and great joy.

Joe Sr. and Rose Kennedy ice skating in Poland Springs, Maine, 1915.

The Kennedys of Boston

The Kennedy family tree is one of deep roots and broad branches, which continue even now to reach far and wide. We are all shaped strongly by our families — our mothers and fathers, sisters, brothers, and grandparents. But John Kennedy was influenced even more than most.

Both of his grandfathers, P.J. Kennedy and John "Honey Fitz" Fitzgerald, were politicians — Irish Catholic politicians in the predominantly Protestant city of Boston, Massachusetts. John's father, Joseph Kennedy, was born in 1888 and married "Honey Fitz's" adored daughter Rose in 1914.

If success can be measured in terms of money, power, and responsibility, Joseph Kennedy was a success. After graduating from Harvard College in 1912, he became the youngest bank president in the country. Not content, he moved on to become the Assistant General Manager of the Bethlehem Steel Company, then a movie producer in the 1920s, and in the 1930s head of the

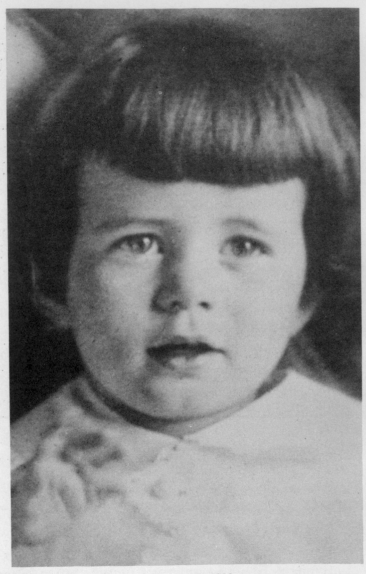

Jack, age 2, 1919.

Securities and Exchange Commission under President Franklin D. Roosevelt.

Before he was thirty-five, Joseph Kennedy had made his first million. At his death, his fortune was estimated somewhere between three and five hundred million dollars. He was a smart businessman. Large companies sought his advice and paid him high fees. He was also a shrewd Wall Street investor who made more money on one stock deal than his father and grandfather had accumulated in their whole lives. Joe Kennedy had come a long way. His son was to go even further. This wouldn't surprise Joe in the least. What would surprise him was which son it turned out to be.

Joe and Rose Kennedy, like many of their Catholic friends, wanted a large family. Joe Jr. was born in July 1915. John Fitzgerald, named after his grandfather, was born May 29, 1917. After that came Rosemary, the first girl, then Kathleen, Eunice, Patricia, Robert, Jean, and finally Edward, called Ted. In the fall of 1914, the Kennedys moved to Brookline, then and now a lovely suburb just far enough but not too far from the center of Boston.

When Joe Jr. and Jack, as John quickly came to be called, were small, their father was often away from home on business. His trips to New York or the West Coast took days and weeks —

not hours as today. But in spite of his long absences, Joe Kennedy never lost sight of his first love, his family. What he didn't provide in quantity of time, he made up in quality of time.

When Jack was just two and a half, he came down with scarlet fever. Today vaccines have wiped out many of these childhood diseases, but in 1920 they were often fatal. Rose had just given birth to Kathleen, so the responsibility of taking care of Jack fell to his father. Joe Sr. proved to be up to the task. He used his influence to get his son admitted to Boston City Hospital. It took some persuasion, since the hospital had a policy of not admitting patients with contagious diseases.

Day after day and week after week, Joe Sr. visited his son. Finally, after four months in the hospital, Jack's illness ran its course, and he was allowed to go home. The nurses who cared for him marveled at how he charmed everyone who came in contact with him. There wasn't a thing the nurses wouldn't do for him, and when he was discharged from the hospital they visited him at home.

Being separated from his home and family at such a young age was a frightening experience. But his father's visits made Jack feel loved and less lonely. Jack's illness brought Joe Sr. closer to all his children. He allowed them into his bedroom for early morning visits, something he hadn't permitted before. It was as if his son's illness had shown Joe Sr. how important it was to appreciate what he had on a daily basis. It was a lesson he had to keep learning but one he would never forget.

After scarlet fever, Jack continued to be ill with one sickness or another. One month it was the mumps, the next whooping cough. Unlike his older brother, who seemed to have been given good health as a gift, Jack was continually sick as a child. His attitude, though, was surprisingly good. He didn't feel sorry for himself. Battling illness was beginning to make Jack Kennedy strong.

But firstborns usually have a special place in their parents' hearts, and it was on Joe Jr. that Joe Sr. pinned his highest hopes. In fact, as soon as Joe Jr. was born, his proud father proclaimed, only half jokingly, "Of course, he's going to be the President of the United States."

Joe Jr. was everything his father had hoped for: good-looking, robust, outgoing, and dedicated. He was fearless — too fearless it would turn out — and he was looked up to by his younger brothers and sisters.

That's the way Joe and Rose planned it. They both felt that bringing up the oldest child properly would make bringing up the rest a lot easier. And it worked. Joe Jr. set the example for his younger

Jack (right) and his older brother, Joe Jr., with their father.

brothers and sisters. But Jack didn't like being number two. When his parents were gone from the house, Joe Jr. automatically assumed authority. Jack rebelled at his rule. Jack was competitive and combative in spite of his frailness and constant problems with health. He ignored them then as he would in the future. Jack was determined to forge his own way, make his own decisions. He challenged his older, healthier brother at every opportunity, and the older they got the more opportunities there were.

One afternoon Joe Jr. suggested to his nine-year-old brother that they race around the block on their bikes. Jack eagerly accepted, looking on any dare as a chance to take a step up the ladder. The boys took off in opposite directions. As they approached the corner where they began, the race turned into a challenge. After the collision Joe Jr. got up, brushed himself off, and walked away. Jack had to have twenty-eight stitches before his wounds would stop bleeding. But he didn't lose. Jack Kennedy didn't like to lose.

The brothers' styles were different. Joe Jr. was always on the go, following his impulsive nature without question. Jack was more cautious. It was as if he were trying to figure out how to get the upper hand with the odds stacked against him. His coughs, fevers, and flus had introduced him to the world of reading — a world he was to love

The two brothers (Jack on the right) at the family's summer house in Hyannis Port, Massachusetts.

and respect all his life. At first his mother read to him: *Sinbad the Sailor, Black Beauty, Peter Pan.* Later he hunted up his own books on heroes and history. During his illnesses, he learned to entertain himself by reading. Jack was more of a reader and a thinker than any of his brothers or sisters.

Although they were serious, Jack's bouts with his older brother took place against a backdrop of family togetherness and harmony. From the very beginning Joe and Rose had decided that they and their children were going to be best friends. Dinnertime was not just a chance for everyone to fill their stomachs, mumble thanks, and set off on the evening's activities. When he was home for dinner, Joe Sr. would be seated at the head of the table. The children were expected to assemble within seconds: the always punctual Joe Jr.; gentle and quiet Rosemary; Kathleen, appropriately called Kick; and Jack, who more than any other Kennedy arrived late.

There was a family rule: Whatever part of the meal had been served before you arrived, you missed. If you arrived just before dessert, that's what you got — dessert, and no more. Unphased, Jack would slip into the kitchen, where the cooks, like the nurses in the hospital, were his biggest fans. They gave him dinner, thinking him one of the sweetest children they had ever met. And it

9

was genuine, both his behavior and their affection. A charming man, Jack Kennedy was first a charming child.

But this was all offstage. On stage at the table, dinner was no laughing matter. Even the somewhat jaunty Jack took his father's orders seriously. The night before, Joe Sr. would have assigned one child a topic, usually politics or government, sometimes history and the people who made it. The instructions were always the same. The child given the assignment was to find out all he or she could by the next night's dinner. The others were to read up on the subject so that they could take part in the discussions. The Kennedys didn't raise onlookers. They didn't believe in watching from the sidelines.

The lively discussions continued throughout much of dinner. But this was no chore. It was fun and exciting, and the children loved it. Government and public service were everyday topics to Jack and his brothers and sisters. It's not far from the truth to say that the Kennedy children went into politics for the same reasons the child of an architect or a doctor or a lawyer becomes one. They grew up hearing about it, liking it, and learning about it.

Quietly, and in her own way, Rose was working just as hard to see that the children grew up the way she felt was proper. Joe Sr. may have presided at the dinner table, but it was Rose who saw to it that all were present and accounted for. The Kennedy household ran like clockwork, and that was no accident. Rose kept an index card for each child. On it was the name, birthday, illnesses, clothing sizes, and any other information she felt was important. And growing up Catholic was important to Rose. Grace was said at every meal, and she insisted on nightly prayers. As their father quizzed and educated the children about politics and government, Rose quizzed and educated them about the Catholic Church. She coached them constantly so that they knew their catechism as well as they knew their own names. Rose believed deeply in the words of St. Luke: "To whom much has been given, much will be required."

Rose taught her children more than religion, however. She took them on short excursions around the neighborhood and on longer trips to many of the historical landmarks that make Boston and its surroundings such a special place. She wanted her children to grow up with a sense of history. And being "Honey Fitz's" daughter, she missed the political atmosphere of Boston. She loved the tree-lined streets of Brookline, but she kept her eyes open for Democratic party rallies and speeches and bundled everyone off to downtown Boston at the drop of a political hat.

Jack's grandfather, "Honey Fitz," the mayor of Boston with President Taft, 1912.

By 1921, when Eunice was born, there were five Kennedy children. Joe Sr. and Rose insisted that school, sports, and other outside activities were never to interfere with family life. This is not true of most families. Even then, in the 1920s, it was probably not true of most. Their parents' rule that nothing come before family — along with the other rules and regulations of growing up a Kennedy — was forming a strong and very special bond among the children.

In 1926 Joe surprised his family by announcing that they were moving to the outskirts of New York City. The dividing lines in Boston were drawn clearly. Joe decided he had had enough of being an outsider in Protestant Boston. Even in Hyannis Port, the small coastal town on Cape Cod, where the family had begun spending their summers, Joe and Rose knew that there were comments made about them behind their backs. Nine-year-old Jack knew none of this and had little sense that he was different from his friends and classmates. In fact, he was right. He wasn't different, something he was to make clear one day in his campaign for the presidency when his religion became a major issue.

But Joe Sr. had felt the prejudice every hour of his life as he was growing up in anti-Irish Boston. He wasn't going to let his children suffer in the same way. Of course, the move to New

York was going to benefit Joe's business — always a big consideration in any decision he made. New York was the financial capital of the country.

With some fears and misgivings, such as any family would suffer, the Kennedys of Boston moved. Unlike most families, however, they made the trip in a private railway car that Joe hired to carry Rose, the children, their governesses, maids, and all their possessions. They moved into a thirteen-room house in the exclusive community of Riverdale, just up the Hudson River from New York City. Riverdale was chosen because it was still countrylike and had good schools. By now Patricia had been born. Bobby was almost a year old and the education of her children was Rose's first concern. Eunice was six, Kathleen seven, Rosemary eight, Jack ten, and Joe Jr. twelve. It was September 1927.

School Days

When the Kennedys were living in Brookline, Jack had started in public school. When he was seven, he had transferred to the Dexter School, a private school for boys, where Joe Jr. was also enrolled. Joe Sr. felt Dexter would be better preparation for college and career. His sons' classmates were the children of wealthy parents, who also wanted only the best for their boys.

Joe Sr. wanted to prepare his sons to live in the world he loved, the world of business and politics. He felt that Catholic school was not that place and his wife's wishes were overruled. Rose was allowed to send the girls, and later Bobby and Teddy, to parochial schools. But as far as *his* two boys were concerned, Joe would hear none of it.

Jack never liked school, at least the going-to-class part. He had trouble keeping his mind on what was being taught. At Dexter the competition

Jack (in front on the right) was a member of the Dexter School's fourth-grade football team.

between the two brothers continued. Somewhat surprisingly, skinny Jack became the quarterback of the football team when he was in the fourth grade. Joe Jr. was irked even more when Jack was also elected captain. Jack thoroughly enjoyed these victories.

When the family moved to New York, the brothers were enrolled at the Riverdale Country Day School. Soon after, Jack went to Canterbury Prep in Rhode Island, but he returned home in the middle of the year with appendicitis. It took a long time for Jack to recover, and he never went back to Canterbury. Instead, in the fall of 1931, he entered The Choate School in Connecticut, where Joe Jr. had already begun to establish a reputation for scholastic excellence. Joe Jr. would be named outstanding senior the year he graduated.

Jack's parents were worried about how well he would do in his courses at Choate. Jack was more concerned about his health. He swam and played football to build up his endurance for the challenge that lay ahead. Joe Sr. and Rose hoped Choate would make Jack see the wisdom of applying himself to his schoolwork and realize that good grades and good work habits would be important to his future success. They hoped having Joe Jr. there to guide him would help.

But going to Choate didn't change Jack's carefree attitude toward his studies. His father was disappointed in his grades. His teachers told Joe Sr. that Jack had the ability, but he just wasn't concentrating on his work. In his first year at Choate he was in the bottom half of his class.

Jack did drive himself to succeed at sports. He swam, played baseball, basketball, crew, and golf. There was hardly a sport in which he didn't compete. He concentrated on making the varsity football team, like his brother. But Jack was thin and lacked the raw strength. He was only able to make the junior varsity squad — a clear disappointment. Although his son's grades worried him, Joe Sr. was impressed with his son's courage.

Then in Jack's junior year, his brother graduated and went off to Harvard University in Cambridge, Massachusetts. Jack felt as if an obstacle had been removed. With his brother gone, he could step into the light. He began to show promise as a writer, and his English teacher suggested he give some thought to a career as a journalist.

But again his health broke down. In the late fall of his junior year, he came home looking pale and had little energy. This time it was hepatitis, a disease of the liver. In February he went into the hospital and was unable to complete the school year. He was so sick his classmates were told to pray for him. But his drive and positive attitude brought him through this latest crisis, and he returned to Choate in September.

Away from his family once again, Jack had the chance to find out who he was. He found that he was smart. Smarter than most. He was always an avid reader. He was the only boy in school who subscribed to *The New York Times*, which he read every day from front to back. He was the best player at "Information Please" a popular radio show of the time that was a kind of quiz show for experts.

Jack discovered, too, that he was popular. His personality attracted people. His friends were loyal and would do anything for him. He seemed to radiate self-confidence, and being around him was exciting. Jack made things happen, unfortunately not always for the best.

When the Headmaster of Choate gave a serious talk about the small percentage of boys who were goof-offs, boys he called "muckers," Jack went into action. With a dozen of his friends he formed The Muckers Club. Almost instantly the Headmaster found out and summoned Joe Sr. to school. The Headmaster explained to Joe Sr., in front of a somewhat worried Jack, that his son was "Public Enemy Number One" and this had to stop. Frankly, he said, he didn't understand how Joe Jr. and Jack could come from the same family.

Joe Sr. was not pleased and assured the Headmaster that it wouldn't happen again. Jack knew he had gone too far, and he knew he'd better not do it again. But he also knew that this prank was something his father could see himself having done in his day. This made all the difference.

Jack enjoyed himself those last two years at Choate. He enjoyed being on his own, and he made friendships that would last him all his life.

Not caring about grades didn't mean he wasn't serious. He was. It was just that quizzes and tests weren't where he wanted to prove himself. Even at eighteen Jack was thinking about the "real" world, the world his father talked about. That was where he wanted to prove himself.

Before he graduated from Choate in 1935, Jack Kennedy's loyal friends voted him "Most Likely to Succeed." They all thought it was a great joke on the school.

During their years at prep school, Joe Jr., Jack, and Kick grew closer and closer till they almost formed a family within a family. The two brothers at Choate and Kathleen in a Catholic school only thirty miles away got to spend a lot of time together. The competition between Joe Jr. and Jack, although always an issue, was not as heated as when they were younger. Jack sympathized with his brother. He saw the responsibilities he had to shoulder, especially when they were home. Joe Sr. was spending a lot of time in California,

The Kennedy family in 1931: (left to right) Bobbie, Jack, Eunice, Jean, Joe Sr., Rose, Pat, Kathleen, Joe Jr., Rosemary and their dog Duddy.

making money and movies. Joe Jr. was the man of the family in his absence. He would spend hours with the younger children, teaching and playing with them. Teddy, born in 1932, was only a baby. But Bobby, shy and awkward, was the only boy in the middle of all the girls — Eunice, Patricia, and Jean. The younger Kennedys looked up to their oldest brother, and Joe Jr. didn't let them down. And for his part, Joe Jr. had come to respect the grit and determination of his younger brother.

There was a Kennedy look that all the children shared, but Jack and Kick looked enough alike to be twins. Not only did they look alike, but they acted alike. They each had a terrific and tireless sense of humor. Kick was fun to be around and made friends easily. Jack would convince his friends to go with him to Kick's school every chance he got. They spent hours talking about school, clothes, parties, and people they knew.

Although they loved nothing more than being silly together, Jack admired Kick for the care and concern she always showed for Rosemary. The sweetest and quietest of the Kennedy children, Rosemary was slow. Slow to walk, slow to talk, and slow to learn the games her brothers and sisters enjoyed together. Gradually and sadly the family came to accept the truth that Rosemary was retarded. First her mother and then Kick made sure Rosemary was included in family activities. Kick made sure Rosemary was never left on the sidelines.

Joe Sr. said that he didn't care if his children agreed with all of his ideas as long as they learned to stand together and come to trust and count on each other.

When Jack graduated, at eighteen, from Choate, he planned to spend a year at The London School of Economics, where Joe Jr. had studied a couple of years earlier. But Jack became sick almost as soon as he got to England. The doctors couldn't agree on what was wrong with him. One said jaundice and another said it was the hepatitis again. Jack returned home to rest and regain his health. Once he felt better, he announced that he wasn't going to Harvard. He was tired of following in someone else's footsteps, although he didn't say it that way. He wanted to go to Princeton with his best friend and Choate classmate, Lem Billings. His parents gave in, but once again Jack's health gave out.

The hepatitis had not been completely cured. Jack tried to hide the fact that he was sick, but he soon had to leave Princeton and check into the hospital. This time for a two-month stay. When he could travel again, his father sent him to Arizona in hopes that the sunny, dry climate would help him regain his health.

Jack, age 20, in Europe with his best friend Lem Billings.

In the fall of 1936, Jack decided he felt well enough to try college once again. This time it would be Harvard, where Joe Jr. was serving on the student council, managing the business side of the yearbook, and getting A's in almost every course. Joe Jr. was already looking forward to law school and a career in politics. His father hadn't been joking when he said Joe Jr. would someday grow up to be President. Father and son were working toward that day.

Jack's grades at Harvard were mediocre, but he became one of the most popular freshmen on campus. He drove himself at sports again. He proved to be a good swimmer, but at six feet one inch and 149 pounds, he was still too frail for football. Of course, Jack wasn't going to be stopped by that, and he insisted on playing. In a scrimmage with the varsity freshmen, Jack went down hard on one play and ruptured a disc in his spine. He would suffer for the rest of his life with back problems.

The next summer he took a trip to Europe with Lem Billings. They went to witness history, and there was plenty to see. The year was 1937. Adolf Hitler was Chancellor of Germany, and the rest of Europe was trying to avoid another war.

In 1938 President Roosevelt appointed Joe Sr. Ambassador to England. In March of that year Joe Sr., ever after called The Ambassador, and the rest of the family sailed for England. Jack was able to join them by the beginning of the summer. These were glorious days for the whole family, but especially for Rose. She was proud of her husband and happy that the whole family would be living under one roof for the first time in years. Joe Jr., Jack, and Kick loved living in London in spite of the threat of war.

Jack was torn between going back to Harvard and staying in England. Joe Jr. had graduated and was in Harvard Law School by then. But Jack longed to stay with his family. They were living in the thirty-six-room embassy residence in England, and they were caught up in the social whirl. The family was invited to all the best parties and to join all the best clubs. They attended the Derby at Epsom Downs, the tennis tournament at Wimbledon, and the Yachting Regatta at Cowes. They spent a weekend with the King and Queen.

As the war clouds that hung over Europe became darker, Jack became increasingly interested in world affairs. He arranged to take a heavier course load in his senior year so he could spend a good part of 1938–39 in England. He also traveled throughout Europe, experiencing the rumblings of war firsthand.

When he returned for his senior year at Harvard, Jack set to work with more intensity than

The Kennedy family (without Joe Jr.) at Vatican City before a special audience with the Pope.

Joe Jr., Kathleen, and Jack in London on September 3, 1939.
They're on their way to hear Great Britain's declaration of war
on Germany.

he had ever shown before. It paid off. He made the dean's list and graduated with honors in June 1940.

But in a way it didn't matter. There were more urgent concerns now. In September 1939, the Germans had invaded Poland. Europe was at war.

In December 1941, three hundred and sixty Japanese bombers would attack the U.S. Pacific fleet at Pearl Harbor, Hawaii. The United States would go to war.

Lt. Kennedy U.S.N.

Jack had graduated from Harvard with honors in political science. His senior thesis, *Appeasement at Munich*, was an analysis of the meeting between Adolf Hitler and England's Prime Minister Neville Chamberlain. It was published in July 1940, by Wilfred Funk, Inc. and sold over 40,000 copies.

In the fall of 1940, Joe Sr. resigned as Ambassador to Great Britain, and the family returned to the States. They moved to a new home in Bronxville, N.Y. but were spending most of their time at their beautiful houses in Palm Beach, Florida, and Hyannis Port. Jack's younger brothers and sisters, older now and all at school, could be joked with as equals. Touch football games were joyously more intense, with victory still the only goal. Jack brought his best friend Lem home with him. Joe Jr. and Kick brought their friends, and the Kennedy family, in a sense, grew larger. Friends were accepted with open arms as long as they played every game, played hard, and didn't

Jack on his June 1940 graduation from Harvard.

mind being the butt of a Kennedy joke. Most didn't.

Jack didn't quite know what to do now that college was over. He thought he might go to Yale Law School, but he changed his mind at the last minute. He went clear across the country instead and enrolled in the Business School at Stanford University in California, where his sister Eunice was a student.

War was beckoning and in his second year, Joe Jr. left Harvard Law School and signed up for the Naval Aviation Cadet Program. Characteristically he chose one of the most difficult branches of the armed forces — only fifty percent of those who signed up in the program made it through.

Soon after, Jack enlisted in the Navy and was assigned to the Office of Naval Intelligence, in Washington, D.C. He hated it. He spent his days sorting bulletins from foreign newspapers. He felt he was just sitting around while there was a war going on. He wasn't a super-patriot, and he didn't romanticize war. He simply wanted to be useful. He asked his father to pull some strings, and in the summer of 1942, he was sent to midshipmen's school in Chicago.

Later, during the ten-week course at training school in Melville, Rhode Island, Jack learned what he had to about piloting a PT (Patrol Torpedo) boat. He was a natural sailor. He had spent his summers sailing at Cape Cod. In March 1943, he sailed to the Solomon Islands, in the South Pacific. Lt. Kennedy was captain of PT 109.

While the war against the Germans raged in Europe and Africa, the Japanese, Germany's ally, were dominating the South Pacific. Japanese destroyers had to be stopped from bringing supplies to their army, which was advancing island by island. PT boats were designed to be fast and maneuverable and to inflict the greatest amount of damage in the shortest amount of time. PT 109 was eighty feet long, made of lightweight plywood, and armed with machine guns, antiaircraft guns and four torpedo tubes. Night after night they patrolled the area, seeing nothing, expecting anything.

Then on the night of August 1, 1943, the waiting was over. The night was heavily overcast, with no moon or stars. Using only one engine, to make as little noise as possible, the patrol encountered four Japanese destroyers.

Lt. Kennedy was at the wheel of PT 109 at 2:30 A.M. when they were rammed by one of the destroyers. The boat was split in two. There was instant chaos as the destroyer disappeared into the night. Two of the crew died immediately. Three were injured and one badly burned. All around the survivors, the water was on fire as the yellow gasoline burned menacingly. They

Jack and his crew on the deck of the PT 109 (Lt. Kennedy is standing on the far right).

clung desperately to the bow of the ship, which had turned over and was floating on its watertight compartments. Jack knew this wouldn't last long. They had to get to land. He directed all but the burned crewman to swim toward an island four miles away.

Taking off his shoes and shirt, Jack took the strap of the nearly unconscious engineer's life-jacket securely between his teeth. Swimming the breaststroke in spurts — going as long as he could and then resting as long as he dared — he arrived at the island five hours later. His crewman was still alive, but Jack was exhausted, nauseous from swallowing salt water, and in agony from the pain in his back. The collision and the strain of swimming with one of his crew in tow had affected the old injury.

After a rest, Jack swam out to sea to try to make contact with a passing PT boat. Not making contact, he decided they had a better chance of being rescued from an island that was closer to the area the PT boats regularly patrolled. In the meantime, they had no water, and their thirst was becoming oppressive.

The next day, the crew made their way to an island a mile and a half away. Jack took the injured crewman in tow again. By then they had had no water or food for seventy-two hours. They drank rain water and ate coconuts and crabs.

Miraculously, they met two inhabitants of the islands. Even more miraculously, the coconut Jack gave them carved with the message:

NUARO ISL
NATIVE KNOWS POSIT
HE CAN PILOT 11 ALIVE NEED
SMALL BOAT
KENNEDY

found its way to the British base on the island. The next day four islanders returned bearing pencilled greetings from the senior British officer in the area. He wrote: "Strongly advise return immediately to here in this canoe." The ordeal was over. And so were Jack's combat days.

Joe and Rose Kennedy heard via radio reports that their son was missing in action. They could do little but wait patiently, although Joe made as many phone calls to Washington as possible. Rose prayed and Joe paced. When word of his rescue reached them, they breathed a sigh of relief and began to look forward to Jack's homecoming.

While Jack was serving in the South Pacific, Joe Jr. was flying B-24 Liberators over the English Channel on the lookout for German submarines. By the spring of 1944, he had flown twenty-four missions, enough to earn him his ticket home.

He refused to be sent home and said he thought he'd stick around till he hit forty.

The war in Europe had been going on for almost five years and the people of England had endured almost daily bombings. The city of London was nearly in ruins. Being under siege had become an everyday occurrence. But the new V-1 rockets being fired on England from concrete bunkers on the coast of German-occupied France came without warning. These buzz-bombs had the tense and tired British population verging on panic. Bold steps had to be taken. Joe Jr. was one of those who volunteered for the job.

A B-24 Liberator was made ready. Everything that wasn't needed to fly or navigate the plane was stripped and replaced with explosives. It would be a one-way trip for the plane. Once the pilot, Joe Jr., had the plane close enough to the bunker that housed the V-1's, he would switch the controls to a "mother ship" flying alongside. The "mother ship" would guide the B-24 by radio signals to the target. The pilot and copilot would parachute to safety. The plane would continue on to the target with no one aboard. It didn't work. On August 12, 1944, just twenty-eight minutes after takeoff, there was an incredible explosion, and Joe Jr. and his copilot were dead.

Joe Sr. was devastated when he received the news. Rose found strength in her religion but was no less shaken. Jack was sad and confused. After years of intense competition, the immovable object had disappeared.

"I'm shadow boxing in a match the shadow is always going to win," he told his best friend, Lem Billings. Jack didn't know where to turn or what to do. He tried to help his father by putting together an album called "As We Remember Joe." His father appreciated the sentiment but couldn't bring himself to look on its pages. Joe Sr. felt that his life had reached its lowest point.

The year was so hideous, Jack couldn't enjoy any of the good things that had happened to him. The PT 109 story had been front page news across the country. He had been awarded a Navy Medal, and people called him a hero. When asked how he had become a hero, he showed that his unfailing sense of humor was still intact. "It was involuntary," he said. "They sank my boat."

When he had returned to the States from the South Pacific, Jack's back had been operated on at a Navy Hospital near Boston. For six months he stayed in the hospital. Then he decided to go to Arizona again to try to regain his health. The malaria he brought back with him from the islands also plagued him.

By mid-1945 Jack's health was somewhat restored. The *Chicago Herald-American*, part of the Hearst newspaper chain, offered him the

Jack receives the Navy and Marine Corp Medal outside of the Chelsea, Mass. Naval Hospital in June 1944.

assignment of covering the upcoming conference in San Francisco, called to establish the United Nations. He spent a month there writing sixteen stories. He enjoyed being a journalist, and he liked to write, but felt frustrated reporting on the news. He wanted to make the news. He gave a lot of thought to his career and talked at length with his father.

By May 1945, the war in Europe was over. The Germans had finally been defeated.

In August 1945, the United States dropped atomic bombs on the cities of Hiroshima and Nagasaki. The Japanese surrendered. The war was over.

Running for Congress

When he was at Choate, and later at Harvard, Jack Kennedy had thought about teaching as a career. He had also been interested in journalism. But the U.N. assignment had shown him that reporting was too much like being on the sidelines, a place he never felt comfortable. He began thinking more seriously about public service — he never liked to call it politics. With Joe Jr. gone, his father urged Jack to run for public office. But Jack wanted it for himself also. His generation had fought a war, and now they were ready to take over the reins of power to preserve the peace.

Jack set his sights on the November 1946 elections and established his official residence on Beacon Street in Boston. He had decided to run for Congress from his grandfather's district, the Eleventh District, which included most of Boston, Cambridge, and the neighboring cities and towns. He set the tone for that campaign and every campaign to come: hard work, late hours, and

Three generations: Jack, his father, and his grandfather "Honey Fitz" (1946).

attention to detail. His campaign theme was "The New Generation Offers a Leader."

Jack Kennedy's critics claimed that his father's money was behind his success. They failed to see that it had more to do with Jack's drive and determination. Every day of the campaign he was the first one up and the last one to bed. He knocked on every door and shook every available hand. His entire family worked for him, as they would in all the campaigns to come. Rose and Eunice arranged house parties and afternoon teas. Jack's opponents laughed at first. But they soon stopped laughing when the voters started lining up to have "tea with the Kennedys."

Jack was considerate. He made sure to thank workers who had labored through the night on his behalf. He sent handwritten apologies if he failed to show up at a reception because his flight was delayed by weather, and he was willing to poke fun at himself. One night at a campaign dinner after the other candidates had finished their tales of Abe Lincoln-like childhoods, he said, "I seem to be the only person who didn't come up the hard way." He smiled the Kennedy smile. He was inviting the audience to be on his side, and they were.

His sensitivity, like his humor, came shining through. Speaking to a group of Gold Star Mothers — women who had lost their sons and daughters in the war — he closed by telling them, "I think I know how all you mothers feel because my mother is a Gold Star Mother, too." His war record was well known, and he was treated like a hero. This was the beginning of the Kennedy magic. He won the election in a landslide. John F. Kennedy was going to Washington, D.C.

Jack and his sister Eunice, who was working for the Justice Department, rented a small house in Georgetown, a part of Washington that looked much like Cambridge and was just minutes away from the Capitol. The thirty–year-old Congressman looked even younger than his years. One day he was actually mistaken for a congressional page when he tried to use the telephones reserved for Congressmen. If he wasn't healthy, he at least looked that way. Spending time with his family at their Palm Beach estate kept him looking tan and fit and ready for work.

His first year in Congress was spent learning the ropes. He served on the Education and Labor Committees and worked for low-cost housing, an area that concerned him greatly. This was a time when millions of veterans were returning home and looking forward to raising families.

Jack Kennedy often showed himself to be unpredictable. He voted against his party if he didn't feel right about Democratic party policy. This won him enemies, but also friends who respected him for his independent thinking. He went on a fact-finding tour of Europe during the summer recess, continuing his self-education in foreign policy.

While in Europe Jack got to see his sister Kick, who had decided to live in England after her British husband was killed in the war. It was a grand reunion. Jack and Kick were best friends and it had been a long time since they had been able to spend so much time together. Sadly, it was the last time they would ever see each other.

Like her brother before her, Kathleen ignored warnings of danger. On May 12, 1948, she was flying to meet her father in Paris. Heavy thunderstorms had grounded all commercial flights. But Kick was flying in a private eight-seater and wasn't bound to obey the airport's recommendation that they wait until the weather cleared. Her plane crashed into a mountain in France, and the Kennedy family was jolted by another tragedy.

Perhaps Jack more than anyone else in the family was affected by Kathleen's death. He had lost a friend. Kick knew what he was like behind the calm exterior. They had trusted and confided in each other since they had been children together. Now he felt shaken and alone. It seemed such a short time since he, Joe Jr., and Kick were the happiest trio alive. Now he alone survived. The realization changed him. Not that day and not that week, but soon after. He became more serious, more dedicated, and more aware that there was no time to waste.

Jack Kennedy soon began planning for an even bigger role in government — Governor of Massachusetts or perhaps U.S. Senator. He worked in Washington on the weekdays and flew to Massachusetts every weekend, racing from town to town and grabbing hamburgers and milk shakes on the run. Sometimes he gave four or five speeches in one town. The number of people who volunteered to work for him grew almost weekly.

Boldly Jack decided on his next step. In 1951 he would run for the Senate against the popular and handsome Republican Senator Henry Cabot Lodge, who was up for reelection. Senator Lodge's family was one of the oldest and most respected in New England. For generations both branches, the Cabots and the Lodges, had produced distinguished citizens, many prominent politicians. Lodge's grandfather had defeated Jack's grandfather in a Senate race thirty-six years earlier. It was a daring decision — the kind that could make or break him. But Jack Kennedy didn't have any time to waste.

It was during the Lodge campaign that Kenny O'Donnell, Larry O'Brien, and Dave Powers joined the Kennedy family, and the "Kennedy Machine" began to form. They became Jack's closest political friends, and they would be with him until the end.

The campaign was bigger, better and, thanks to Bobby, more organized than the first. Bobby, who was a lawyer working with the Justice Department, left his job to take over the campaign. He was just twenty-six, but he was forceful and decisive and there wasn't anything he wouldn't do for his brother. Under his steady hand the campaign moved forward.

Lodge underestimated Jack Kennedy from the beginning, and he lost by over seventy thousand votes. Dwight Eisenhower, who won the presidency in a landslide, spent the day before the election in Boston campaigning for Lodge. But he was unable to pull Republican Lodge in on his coattails. Jack won. It was a head–turning display of vote–getting ability.

Congressman Kennedy was now Senator Kennedy.

Some of Jack's friends felt that when he was introduced to Jacqueline Bouvier he had finally met his match. Jack and Jackie were alike in many ways. Each had been raised in an environment of wealth and privilege. They were good at keeping up appearances and looking unruffled at all times. People who knew them described them as two icebergs because such a small part of their characters was visible to the outside world.

The bride and bridegroom on their wedding day, September 12, 1953. Jack married Jacqueline Bouvier in Newport, Rhode Island.

Jackie was only twenty-one when they met. Jack was thirty-four. She had been raised on Park Avenue and Southhampton, Long Island. She had been sent to the best girls' schools. She was Catholic. She was pretty, tall, and graceful.

At the time they met, she was the "Inquiring Photographer" for *The Washington Times-Herald*. She interviewed Jack Kennedy, asking him how he would describe himself and what his best and worst qualities were. The answers: "an idealist without illusions" and "curiosity and irritability."

Jack was a popular Washington bachelor, but the more he dated Jackie the more convinced he became that she was special. In May 1953, he proposed and a few months later, on September 12, they were married in Newport, Rhode Island. Thousands of spectators waited outside the church to get a closer look at the bride and groom.

By early 1954, Jack's health had become an issue once again. The pain in his back was so bad that he was forced to use crutches much of the time, although he would never use them in public. He entered the Hospital for Special Surgery in New York on October 21. The operation was long and difficult. So was his convalescence. Twice infections set in, and his family was summoned. He was so ill he was given the "last rites" of the

Catholic Church. But once again he was able to rally. In mid-December, he and Jackie flew to Palm Beach to be with his family and recuperate. It was a brief stay. By January he had to return for a second operation. A month later he returned to Palm Beach.

The seven months Jack spent recovering in Palm Beach were difficult for him. He had nothing but time on his hands. He was surrounded by books and magazines and the idea for a magazine article on political courage began to take shape. It was a subject that was very much on his mind. He had received some sharp criticism from his fellow Democrats for the positions he took on certain issues. Unable to sleep more than an hour at a time, he started work on the article. Soon it grew into a book. It was a collection of essays on eight political figures who had the courage to stand up for unpopular causes they felt were right and just. Among them were John Quincy Adams of Massachusetts and Thomas Hart Benton of Missouri.

Profiles in Courage became Jack's second and biggest bestseller. Over the next two years it sold a hundred and twenty-five thousand copies. In 1957 he received a Pulitzer Prize for the book, which earned him a reputation as a scholar in addition to the reputation he was building as a statesman.

In May 1955, he finally returned to his Senate office. His back had improved, but he had to wear a lift in his left shoe and a brace. He swam and did exercises daily to strengthen his back. He also discovered the wonderful comforts of a rocking chair.

Shortly after he settled back to work, he was asked to narrate a film being prepared for the 1956 Democratic Convention. The film and Jack's nominating speech for Adlai Stevenson, the Democratic candidate for president that year, were shown on national television. Both were a resounding success for Jack.

The 1956 Democratic Convention was the first in which television played a real part in the selection of a president and a vice president. Television connected people instantly. The delegates were influenced by what they saw. The voters back home called them to give their reactions to what they were seeing in their living rooms. It was an "information loop" that would change the way American politics was conducted in the future. Jack Kennedy was the first politician it affected.

"Who's this Kennedy," everyone wanted to know. A spontaneous movement to nominate him for vice president began to sweep across the convention floor. Jack lost, but it was close. With no planning or organization he had very nearly

Kennedy supporters at the 1956 Democratic Convention in
Chicago demonstrate for Jack's nomination as Vice-President.

been nominated for vice president. From that day on, everything Jack did was directed toward the 1960 Convention. And it wasn't the vice presidency he was interested in.

Back in Washington, Jack worked more closely with the party "big wigs," anxious to have their support. Bobby worked with the Stevenson campaign, not only to help elect his party's nominee, but to gain experience in a presidential election campaign. Jack's fellow senators viewed him much differently now. Added to the luster of the Pulitzer Prize was the notoriety he had gained with the television coverage. He was not only the senator from Massachusetts, but a possible candidate for president in 1960.

Jack Kennedy had become a national figure. He accepted as many speaking engagements across the country as he could. As a hardworking legislator, he sponsored a labor-reform bill to curb corruption in labor unions, and he became a member of the Senate Foreign Relations Committee. He would always be grateful to Senate Majority Leader Lyndon Baines Johnson for giving him a seat on that committee.

In 1958 he ran for reelection to the Senate. It was an off year — no one was running for president — and it would be difficult to get voters to turn out. The "Kennedy Machine" worked hard in Massachusetts and close to two million people voted. It was a record. Even more impressive was Jack's margin of victory. He won by eight hundred and seventy-five thousand votes, the largest margin in any senatorial election.

In January 1960, John F. Kennedy announced publicly that he was a candidate for the Democratic presidential nomination. He decided to run in as many state primaries as possible. The primaries were where he had to gain enough delegates to win his party's nomination. The nomination would be decided when the delegates met at the Democratic National Convention in the summer.

Primaries are even more important when there is no favorite. In 1960 the race for the nomination was far from settled. Senators Hubert Humphrey of Minnesota and Estes Kefauver of Tennessee were also candidates. Jack felt he had to show that he could get votes outside of Massachusetts. And he also wanted to show that his religion would not be an obstacle to his election. Americans had never elected a Catholic president.

New Hampshire held the first primary. Jack won, but his victory in this New England state wasn't surprising. The next primary was only a month later in Wisconsin, Senator Humphrey's neighboring state. The weather was bitter cold, and the primary was bitterly contested.

The Kennedy family swarmed all over the state,

ignoring the cold and snow. They gave teas and receptions; they spoke at lodges and factories and appeared in supermarkets and shopping malls. Jack's determination was never stronger. One day as he was shaking hands and battling his way through knee-high snow in a small Wisconsin town, an elderly woman stopped him. "You're too soon, my boy, too soon," she said. Jack smiled at her and shook his head. "No, this is my time," he said. "My time is now."

Although he won in Wisconsin, his victory was not big enough to force Humphrey out of the race. The next stop was West Virginia. It would prove to be the turning point in Jack Kennedy's race for the nomination.

West Virginia was a state with very few Catholics. A victory there would mean that Jack was not just popular with Catholics. He tackled the religious issue head on. "No one asked me if I was Catholic when I joined the U.S. Navy," he told his West Virginia audiences. National newspapers and network television cameras picked this up, and in the coming weeks Jack's religion became a much less important issue.

Jack won in West Virginia, and in the weeks following he won in Maryland, Indiana, Oregon, and Nebraska. It was an impressive showing, not only to voters who like a winner, but to his fellow Democrats. To them the most important qualifi-

Jack and his vice-presidential running mate, Texas Senator Lyndon Johnson.

cation a presidential nominee needed was the ability to win. It looked like John F. Kennedy could win in November.

By the time the 1960 Democratic National Convention opened on July 11 in Los Angeles, Jack's primary victories had brought him close to securing the nomination on the first ballot. Five hundred and fifty delegates were pledged to Kennedy. He needed only two hundred and eleven more to get the nomination. But Adlai Stevenson's supporters still hoped their candidate could win. When Senator Eugene McCarthy placed Stevenson's name in nomination, the convention hall erupted in cheers for a full half hour. But the efforts Jack and his staff had made in the primaries paid off. In the roll call of states, Wyoming gave Jack the delegates he needed to win the nomination.

Jack immediately turned his attention to the choice of a vice presidential running mate. He shocked his staff and supporters, as well as Lyndon Johnson himself, when he offered the spot to the Texas senator. Johnson was considered too conservative by most of Jack's advisors. His reasons for choosing Johnson were complicated, but the deciding factor was probably the need to have someone on the Democratic ticket who could win Texas and some of the southern states. Lyndon Johnson was that man.

On Friday, July 5, Jack Kennedy delivered his acceptance speech at the convention. He was a very different person from the man who went to Washington thirteen years earlier.

Politically he was considered a liberal, although many of his fellow Congressmen had more liberal voting records. He was independent. He didn't decide every issue on the basis of party. He wanted to do what was right and felt that what was right would be the best thing politically.

He surprised people with his intensity and disarmed them with his easy charm. People came away from a meeting with Jack Kennedy liking him more than they thought they would. He was witty and intelligent. He didn't talk down to people or over their heads. He appeared strong, yet patient, cool and unflappable while still managing to look a touch shy. He seemed to have more style than other politicians. He had what the news media were soon to call "charisma."

Kennedy for President

When Jack Kennedy was the junior senator from Massachusetts, he was friendly with his colleague across the hall — the Republican senator from California. When he returned to his Senate office in May 1955, after one of his back operations, he was pleased to find a bouquet of flowers waiting for him. The card read: "Welcome home — Dick Nixon." Now he and Richard Nixon would engage in one of the most dramatic presidential races in American political history.

It didn't take long for the campaign to reach its high point. On September 25, 1960, seventy million Americans watched the first of four debates on television. Jack Kennedy had agreed immediately when the idea for the debates was proposed by NBC. Richard Nixon, who had been Eisenhower's vice president for two terms, made experience one of the major issues of the campaign. Jack was eager to show that he was not too young or inexperienced to be president. He saw the debates as an opportunity to disprove the Nixon charge.

The first debate, in Chicago, was confined to domestic issues — government spending, farm policy, civil rights, and other special concerns. If you read a transcript of the debate you would probably consider it a draw. But the debate was seen, not read. What the television viewers saw was a dark, tired, perspiring Nixon. Jack Kennedy was a startling contrast. He seemed relaxed, in control, well informed. No matter what the topic, he looked cool and calm — exactly the qualities people look for in their leaders. Richard Nixon's answers were long, sometimes rambling. He seemed uncertain, nervous.

During the next three debates the contrast was not as dramatic, but it was there. Television, which had played such a major role in the selection of a vice presidential candidate in 1956, was now playing an even more crucial role in choosing a president.

The Republicans' charge of youth and inexperience was no longer an issue. Contributions to the Kennedy campaign increased dramatically. Volunteers from every state offered to work for the candidate who had inspired their trust and confidence. The 1960 Kennedy presidential campaign was starting to roll. But Richard Nixon had been Vice President, and no one on the Kennedy

Senator and Mrs. Kennedy meet Vice-President Richard Nixon in 1959.

Democrat Jack Kennedy and Republican Richard Nixon, the two candidates for President, debate the issues on national television.

staff, least of all the candidate, was going to take anything for granted. Besides, the Gallup poll showed voters prefering Nixon to Kennedy fifty-three percent to forty-seven percent.

Jack traveled to two hundred and thirty-seven cities. His appearances were well planned in advance. Airport crowds were huge and enthusiastic. They waved handmade signs and marched to the sound of high school bands.

By mid-October, young people, many of whom had never participated in politics before, were getting involved. Colleges and college towns were becoming Kennedy strongholds.

On October 27, the following article appeared in *The New York Times*:

Senator John F. Kennedy telephoned Mrs. (Martin Luther) King in Atlanta to express concern over the jailing of her husband. "Senator Kennedy said he was very much concerned about both of us," Mrs. King said. "He said this must be hard on me. He wanted me to know he was thinking about us, and he would do all he could to help. I told him I appreciated it and hoped he would help," she said.

In Atlanta, it was reported that Republican headquarters had asked for some kind of statement on the King case from Vice President Nixon or from Republican campaign officials. An aide said the Vice President would have no comment.

The Reverend Martin Luther King Jr.'s campaign of civil disobedience had gotten him arrested. He encouraged blacks in the South to refuse to go to the back of a bus because the front seats, even if empty, were reserved for white people. And he supported those who refused to leave "white only" lunch counters until they were served. Word of Kennedy's thoughtful call to Mrs. King spread quickly throughout the black communities in the United States.

Then one week later, Jack Kennedy unveiled his proposal for a "peace corps" — an army of young people who would volunteer two years of their lives fighting poverty and disease around the world. They might be sent to Malaya, India, or Venezuela. The idea was new and exciting. Today the Peace Corps is an independent agency of the government and has placed more than 100,000 volunteers in over sixty countries.

It looked as if Jack was doing things right. Indeed, it seemed his time was now. Still, the Kennedy campaigners, the family, and loyal staff didn't let up. They worked on getting out the vote. As the campaign wound down to the final days, the election was considered to be very close.

On November 8, Jack and his family gathered at the Kennedy compound in Hyannis Port, where he and Bobby had houses near their parents. Everyone went to Bobby's house, which was more of a command post than a home. They camped in front of the TV and waited.

The election was very close. When Nixon took the lead everyone murmured, "It's too early to tell." When Jack took the lead, it was declared a trend. At 7:15 P.M. CBS predicted a Nixon victory. But Jack and Bobby knew better. Four key states — Michigan, Minnesota, California, and Illinois — were still too close to call.

At three o'clock in the morning, Jack had 261 electoral votes. He was just 8 short of victory. He decided to go to bed. While he was sleeping he lost California. But he won Illinois, Michigan, Minnesota, and New Mexico, gaining 303 electoral votes and the Presidency of the United States. Richard Nixon actually won more states than Jack Kennedy, but he got only 219 electoral votes. Out of the 68,832,818 total votes cast, Jack Kennedy won by only 118,550.

At seven o'clock in the morning, Secret Service agents were in Hyannis Port to protect the President-elect. In January the Kennedy family — Caroline, who was three and John Jr. who had been born just two weeks after his father's election — moved into the White House.

In the White House

The night before the inauguration, eight inches of snow fell on the nation's capital, giving it an other-worldly look.

The morning of the inauguration, the sky was blue and cloudless. The air felt electric as the temperature barely reached the twenties. The crowds of people who began lining the parade route in the early morning hours shifted from side to side, stamping their feet and clapping their gloved hands. Despite the cold and wind, they waited patiently to get a glimpse of their new President and his wife. The brilliant yellow-white sun seemed to be a sign that the future would be bright.

The crowds watched and waited as poet Robert Frost struggled in the wind and the glare of the sun to read the brief dedication he had written especially for the occasion. Lyndon Johnson stepped forward, offering his hat as a shield. But after reading only three lines, Frost put aside the dedication and recited his poem "The Gift Out-right" from memory.

The President-elect was sworn in by Earl Warren, the Chief Justice of the Supreme Court. Then the President stepped forward to deliver his Inaugural Address. John Kennedy began in the chopped cadence and Boston accent that was now familiar:

> We observe today not a victory of party but a celebration of freedom, symbolizing an end as well as a beginning, signifying renewal as well as change. For I have sworn before you and Almighty God the same solemn oath our forebears prescribed nearly a century and three-quarters ago . . .
>
> The world is very different now. For man holds in his mortal hands the power to abolish all forms of human poverty and all forms of human life. And yet the same revolutionary belief for which our forebears fought is still at issue around the globe, the belief that the rights of man come not from the generosity of the state but from the hand of God . . .
>
> We dare not forget today that we are the heirs of that first revolution. Let the word go forth from this time and place, to friend

January 20, 1960: Jack gives his inauguration speech.

and foe alike, that the torch has been passed to a new generation of Americans, born in this century, tempered by war, disciplined by a hard and bitter peace, proud of our ancient heritage, and unwilling to witness or permit the slow undoing of these human rights to which this nation has always been committed, and to which we are committed today at home and around the world.

President Kennedy gave one of the shortest speeches in inaugural history, but many thought it one of the best. A simple sentence toward the end of the speech is remembered today more than any other. It begins:

And so my fellow Americans, ask not what your country can do for you; ask what you can do for your country.

A new generation was taking over. A generation that had seen war and wanted no more. A generation of ideas and ideals, of action and compassion, who would lead us to a brave new world.

Unfortunately the feeling that all would be well, that everything was now possible, did not last long. President Kennedy had announced his cabinet appointments before he took office: Dean Rusk, secretary of state; Robert McNamara, secretary of defense; Douglas Dillon, a Republican, secretary of the treasury. In general the reaction was favorable. His choice of attorney general, however, raised a few eyebrows. The reaction was anticipated and Jack used his favorite weapon — humor. At a dinner he told his audience he "thought Bobby should have some government legal experience before going into private practice."

The humor covered up Jack's determination to have his brother as his attorney general. He had a high regard for Bobby's ability to get things done. But more importantly, he wanted someone on his staff to give him the bad news as well as the good. Someone who would tell him when he was wrong as well as when he was right. He knew he could count on Bobby to do this. As time passed, the eyebrows were lowered, but the eyes kept careful watch.

The President held his first televised news conference a few weeks after he took office. Standing at the podium, at ease before the cameras and the 418 reporters, he delivered answers that were entertaining and enlightening. The public and the press were captivated, and a Kennedy news conference became something not to be missed.

Then, very early in 1961, President Kennedy ran headlong into his first crisis.

President Kennedy with his brother Attorney General Robert F. Kennedy at the White House.

In November 1960, the President-elect's staff had been briefed by President Eisenhower's aides. Cuba had been high up on the agenda. Ninety miles off the coast of Florida, this island was ruled by Fidel Castro, who had led a rebellion that ousted the country's dictator in 1958. Castro was extremely anti-American and very friendly with the Russians.

The Eisenhower aides explained that the Central Intelligence Agency of the United States had been working with many of the Cubans who fled their country when Castro took over. Fourteen hundred of these exiles were being trained secretly by the CIA in Guatemala in preparation for an invasion of Cuba. They hoped the invasion would result in a popular uprising that would overthrow Castro. United States backing for the invasion was kept secret from the Congress. In early March the President of Guatemala notified the U.S. Government that the presence of the Cuban exiles was an embarrassment to him and his country. They had to be gone by the end of April.

The President met with Dean Rusk, Robert McNamara, members of the CIA, and the Joint Chiefs of Staff. The President listened to all the facts and recommendations. There were numerous discussions on the pros and cons of canceling the invasion. Although the President had his doubts about the wisdom of the plan, he felt there were many reasons to go through with it. Intelligence information reported that Castro's military strength was growing at such a rapid rate that it was now or never. To back out now, after a year of preparation and training, would allow Kennedy's critics to attack him as "soft" on communist Cuba. With grave misgivings Kennedy gave the go-ahead for the invasion.

On the morning of April 17, the army of 1,400 Cuban exiles attempted a landing on the beaches of the Bay of Pigs. They were met by over 20,000 of Castro's soldiers. The invasion had come as no surprise to Castro. To make matters worse, air cover for the landing party proved ineffective. Those men who managed to scramble ashore alive were captured. There was no popular uprising — indeed, there was hardly time. The invasion was over as soon as it had started.

The invasion was a public humiliation for the new administration. President Kennedy took full blame for the Bay of Pigs disaster. "There's an old saying," he said. "Victory has a hundred fathers and defeat is an orphan."

In late May, the President flew to Vienna for an important summit meeting with Premier Nikita Khruschev, head of the Soviet Union. The meeting was as much a test of personalities as a debate

President Kennedy meets with the head of the Soviet Union, Nikita Khrushchev.

on the issues — much to Jack Kennedy's displeasure. There were lengthy discussions on the expansion of communism outside of the Soviet Union, space exploration, and the control of nuclear arms. For the President the issue was broader: How could two nations with such different ways of governing themselves co-exist peacefully?

The burly, brusque Soviet leader tried to bully the younger man. The President was impressed with Khruschev's debating ability, and Khruschev left the meeting respecting his adversary. An important personal relationship was beginning to grow between the two leaders. This relationship would play a crucial role in world affairs in the months to come.

The President had just returned from the summit meeting with Premier Khruschev when there were rumblings of a new crisis.

At the end of World War II, Germany had been divided into two sectors: East and West. The East came under the influence of the Soviet Union, the West under the influence of the United States and her allies.

Berlin, the former capital of Germany, was also divided into East and West. Lying within East German territory, it was a cause of concern. This state of tension between the U.S. and the Soviet Union came close to but never involved combat.

Instead the world entered into what came to be called the cold war. In 1948 the Soviets blocked all land access to West Berlin. The U. S. and her allies flew in food and supplies for 321 days until the blockade was withdrawn.

Now, in the summer of 1961, the cold war was heating up again. East Berliners had been crossing into West Berlin in increasing numbers. In July 30,000 people left East Berlin to live in the West. The Chancellor of East Germany was threatening to shut down air traffic to the West. Tension was building daily. The President had little choice but to wait for the Soviets' next move. He was sympathetic to those on his staff who felt that Khruschev was using this as a test case. They advised a hard stand at any cost. Berlin dominated the President's conversations that whole summer. Although President Kennedy hoped for a peaceful settlement of the Berlin situation, he knew that if he didn't appear firm, the Soviet Union might become more aggressive. On July 25, he gave a nationally televised speech in which he said:

We cannot and will not permit the Communists to drive us out of Berlin. . . . For the fulfillment of our pledge to that city is essential to the morale and security of Western Germany, to the unity of Western Europe, and to the faith of the entire free world . . .

we will at all times be ready to talk, if talk will help . . . we seek peace, but shall not surrender.

Two weeks later, Khruschev replied on Soviet television. He promised, as President Kennedy had, to seek peaceful solutions while being prepared for military intervention. It was a serious test of wills.

One week later, East German troops and police began occupying most of the border crossing points. In the days that followed, they tore up the streets, put up road blocks, and stretched barbed wire everywhere. Windows of buildings lining the border were bricked up. The building of the Berlin Wall had begun.

The President wanted the people of Berlin and the world at large to know that we would not abandon them. The European alliance that the U.S. had tried to build since the end of the war was at stake. West Berlin's mayor, Willy Brandt, asked President Kennedy to act firmly and decisively. Vice President Lyndon Johnson was dispatched to West Berlin. At the same time, the President ordered 1,500 troops into the city. The Vice President's presence was effective and, although the Wall remained, there were no further steps taken by the Soviet Union in Berlin.

Two years later, President Kennedy would visit

Jack in West Berlin, 1963, where he gave his now famous *Ich bin ein Berliner* speech.

West Germany to give his personal assurance of the U.S. commitment. "For your safety is our safety, your liberty is our liberty . . ." he told the enthusiastic crowds that greeted him in Bonn, the capital. The crowds were equally enthusiastic in Frankfurt, but the largest crowds were waiting in West Berlin. Half of the city's population of two and a third million had turned out. The President spoke so near the Wall that he could have peered into East Berlin if it were not for the huge banners that had been hung by the East Germans to block his view.

"All free men, wherever they live, are citizens of Berlin," he said. "And therefore, as a free man, I take pride in the words *Ich bin ein Berliner* — I am a Berliner." The crowds erupted in cheers. It seemed as if they would never stop.

But in 1961, the President was concerned with what he saw as another possible battleground between the U.S. and the U.S.S.R. — space. He addressed the United Nations saying, "The cold reaches of the universe must not become an arena of an even colder war."

The U.S. space program lagged far behind the Soviet Union's. In 1957 the Soviets had launched the first space satellite, Sputnik I. On April 12, 1961, Yuri Gagarin, a Russian, became the first man to travel in space. He orbited the earth in less than two hours.

In a special State of the Union speech in May 1961, President Kennedy committed the United States to landing a man on the moon and returning him safely to earth "before this decade is out."

In May 1961, Commander Alan Shepard Jr. became the first American successfully launched into space. He traveled 115 miles above the earth and back. In February 1962, John Glenn became the first American to orbit the earth. In the three years of the Kennedy Administration, the National Aeronautics and Space Administration (NASA) put twenty-five satellites into orbit. The President had shifted "our efforts in space from low to high gear."

As a result, on July 20, 1969, at 10:26 P.M. (EDT) Neil A. Armstrong, an American, became the first man to walk on the moon.

During this first crisis-filled year, Jackie Kennedy set about establishing her own philosophy and style. She disliked being called the First Lady. She said it made her sound like a saddle horse. She turned her attention first to redecorating the top floors of the White House, where the family rooms were located. A kitchen was installed on the same floor as the children's bedrooms, so a sense of home and family could be

Halloween in the President's office, Caroline and John-John in
costume.

maintained. Quiet and shy herself, she wanted her children to have the most normal childhood possible. A playground and treehouse turned the south lawn into a backyard. There were pets of all sorts — horses, dogs, ducks, and hamsters — that could be found anywhere at anytime. The Kennedys had lunch together in the family quarters as often as possible. When they weren't officially busy at night, Jack loved to watch movies, especially comedies and history, with his family and friends.

The part of the White House that was open to the public was Jackie's next concern. She formed a Fine Arts Committee to look for antiques to refurnish the White House in the various periods of past Presidents. To help raise funds to finance this effort, she wrote a guidebook that sold for a dollar. During her first year in the White House, a record number of tourists came to visit. On Valentine's Day in 1962, CBS televised a proud Mrs. Kennedy giving America a tour of the White House.

October 1, 1962: James Meredith registers for classes at the University of Mississippi while 1,400 U.S. marshalls and soldiers stand guard.

Days of Crisis

The civil rights cause had won an important victory in 1954, when the Supreme Court said that "separate but equal" education was discriminatory. For the first time segregation in education was against the law.

During John F. Kennedy's presidency, there was a sharp increase in the number of school districts that were desegregated. There were many bitter disputes, but the climactic case came with James Meredith's request for admission to the University of Mississippi at Oxford for the 1962 fall term. On his application he wrote:

I am an American-Mississippi-Negro citizen. With all of the recurring events regarding changes in our educational system taking place in our country in this new age I feel certain that this application does not come as a surprise to you. I certainly hope that this matter will be handled in a manner that will be complimentary to the University and to the State of Mississippi. Of course, I am the one that will, no doubt, suffer the greatest consequences of this event.

The admissions office of the University had no intention of handling his application in a manner that was "complimentary to the University." They rejected James Meredith's application on academic grounds. The Federal Courts ruled that he was rejected on racial grounds and that he must be admitted. The governor of Mississippi refused. Meredith, accompanied by U.S. marshalls, was turned away at the door of the University by the governor and an angry mob. Ironically, two days later the country would celebrate the one hundreth anniversary of Lincoln's Emancipation Proclamation, which declared that slavery would no longer be tolerated in the South — the first step on the long road to equal rights for black Americans.

The governor of Mississippi continued to defy the courts, but Robert Kennedy, the attorney general, refused to be put off the course set by his brother. The governor told the attorney general that Mississippians would raise enough money to send Meredith to any university he wanted to attend, provided it was outside the state.

After numerous attempts at negotiation, the Mississippi National Guard was mobilized and

U.S. Army troops were sent to Oxford on the orders of the President.

The marshalls and the deputy attorney general of the United States were successful in getting Meredith inside the building. But the crowd, estimated at 2,500 began throwing bottles and bricks. As the southern afternoon turned to dusk, shotguns and rifles were spotted in the crowd and the marshalls began to use tear gas. The confrontation continued, and the National Guard and the Army troops were ordered to move in. The clash that resulted left two dead and hundreds wounded. But James Meredith became the first black student admitted to the University of Mississippi.

The President battled a stubborn Congress as he struggled to get his civil rights bill passed. He wanted to end discrimination in public housing, in schools, unions, and businesses — wherever federal funding was involved. It was a sweeping bill. But the President knew how to count votes in Congress as well as anyone, and he knew its chances were small.

On August 28, 1963, 250,000 people, black and white, marched on the nation's capital to demand civil rights. It was an orderly, dignified, and profound protest. A true turning point in American history. Speaking to the marchers gathered in front of the Lincoln Memorial, Dr. Martin Luther King Jr. made his now famous "I have a

Black and white Americans march on the nation's capital to demand civil rights. Dr. Martin Luther King Jr. is in the center, front row.

dream" speech. The civil rights bill was Jack Kennedy's dream, and his inability to get Congress to pass it was his biggest disappointment.

For many Americans, 1962 would be remembered for the thirteen days at the end of October when they watched the skies for enemy planes and missiles; when families discussed where each of them would go when the attack came. October was the time of the Cuban Missile Crisis. A time when the world came closer to a nuclear war than it has before or since. And it all happened within thirteen tense days.

On Tuesday morning, October 16, the President was shown aerial photographs of Soviet-made nuclear missiles being installed in Cuba. The President was urged by many of his advisors to attack and destroy the missiles. The President chose a less belligerent course. At 7:00 P.M. on Monday, October 22, President Kennedy went on national television and announced that:

All ships of any kind bound for Cuba from whatever nation or port will, if found to contain cargoes of offensive weapons, be turned back . . .

It shall be the policy of this nation to regard any nuclear missile launched from Cuba against

The Kennedy's relax at Hyannis Port with a few furry friends.

Jack always enjoyed sailing.

any nation in the Western Hemisphere as an attack by the Soviet Union on the United States, requiring a full retaliatory response upon the Soviet Union.

On Wednesday morning, October 24, the blockade went into effect as twenty-five Soviet merchant ships continued steaming toward Cuba. The ships were scheduled to be intercepted at 10:30 A.M. The President and the country watched and waited. At 10:25 A.M. the Soviet ships stopped dead in the water. The blockade had worked. On Sunday, October 28, just thirteen days after they had been discovered, Soviet Premier Khruschev agreed to dismantle and remove all missiles.

By his third year in office, Jack Kennedy had begun to feel more comfortable as President. He was spending more weekends at Camp David, the presidential retreat in Maryland. The crisp air and quiet surroundings were a welcome change from the pressure back at the capital. He swam in the heated pool, played on a three hole golf course, and often kept an eye on John-John while Jackie and Caroline went horseback riding.

When a reporter once asked the President why he liked his job so much, he replied, "Well, I find the work rewarding...the Greek definition of happiness is the full use of your powers along lines of excellence. I find, therefore, that the Presidency provides some happiness."

In 1963 the President's concern was growing about a small country halfway around the world. It was a place that most Americans had never heard of. Soon it would become a place Americans would never forget. It was called Vietnam.

Vietnam was part of what was once called French Indochina. The French were forced to withdraw in 1954 after seventy years of colonial rule. They left a country divided into North and South. The North was led by Ho Chi Minh, a communist, and the South by Ngo Dinh Diem. The United States supported Diem and hoped that he would govern the South in a way that would unite the people and prevent the expansion of communism in that part of the world.

The President knew that military might alone would not win in Vietnam. He knew that the people had to believe in their government. He sent Vice President Johnson to Vietnam to talk to Diem about the long-awaited reforms in education, farming, and agriculture. The Vice President reported that the time had come to either pull out or give full support. President Kennedy was unwilling to risk the danger of a communist takeover, which he was sure would result from an American withdrawl. He ordered a buildup of American military "advisors."

On November 1, 1963, Diem was murdered by his generals. There were now sixteen thousand American troops in South Vietnam. The President was growing more skeptical of the road he was traveling. He ordered a symbolic withdrawal of American troops — a thousand men. But the ordered withdrawal was never put into effect. On Friday, November 22, 1963, the President was in Dallas, Texas.

By the fall of 1963, Jack was already campaigning for re-election.

November 22, 1963

By late 1963, the President had his eye on the 1964 election. In September he toured the Midwest, visiting many of the states he lost in 1960. He had not done well in the South, either. Even with Lyndon Johnson on the ticket, Kennedy had only narrowly won Texas, and over sixty-two percent of the citizens of Dallas voted against him.

Although many of those closest to the President were opposed to the trip, the President agreed to visit Dallas on November 22. During the 1960 campaign, crowds in Dallas had spit on Lyndon Johnson, their former senator. And Adlai Stevenson had been assaulted by unruly Dallas crowds on United Nations Day. The city was known to be in "a right-wing mood." More homicides were committed in Texas than in any other state in the union — and more in Dallas than anywhere else in the state.

The President was aware of the situation, but he had always confronted adversity with courage.

He had no intention of stopping now. If he was to win the 1964 election, voters in the South and Texas would have to join his campaign. There was still a great deal Jack Kennedy wanted to accomplish as President. He looked forward to continuing to build peaceful relationships with the Soviet Union, making the U.S. first in space, expanding the Peace Corps, and continuing to push the cause of civil rights.

Jack Kennedy felt he had weathered the worst storms. From the humiliation of the Bay of Pigs he had gone on to represent an America that stood fast when necessary, but always held out the olive branch of peace. The nuclear test ban treaty that had been signed only weeks before was proof of these efforts. Even his critics had been impressed with his growth, determination, and wisdom during three crisis-ridden years. The country's love affair with their confident, articulate, charming leader was still in full bloom.

The President looked forward to campaigning again. He enjoyed getting out from behind his desk and meeting the people face to face, and he always felt invigorated after a good campaign trip. The trip to Texas was so important that Jackie agreed to accompany him. It was the first time she had ever gone on a presidential campaign trip. Her presence caused excitement, for by now she was as popular as her husband.

Dallas, Texas, November 22, 1963.

President and Mrs. Kennedy were greeted by large, friendly crowds in San Antonio, Houston, and Fort Worth. At the Dallas airport the crowds were fifteen deep and security was tight. For the first time in their Texas trip they saw hostile signs — HELP KENNEDY STAMP OUT DEMOCRACY; YANKEE GO HOME AND TAKE YOUR EQUALS WITH YOU — held aloft by some of the people lining the motorcade route.

The President and Mrs. Kennedy sat in the backseat of the President's Lincoln convertible. Governor and Mrs. Connolly waved from the seats directly in front of them. The rain had stopped and there was no need to put up the bubbletop. Now everyone could get a good look at the President and his beautiful wife.

The Lincoln was traveling at 11.2 miles per hour as it negotiated the curves in the highway that ran past the Texas Book Depository building. Lee Harvey Oswald was waiting in a sixth floor corner window of the building, holding a rifle. The unhappy and confused Oswald had just returned from the Soviet Union, where he had hoped to find a better life in a communist society. As an ex-marine he was an expert marksman. At 12:30 P.M. President Kennedy was hit by a bullet fired from Oswald's rifle. Governor Connolly was also hit. Five seconds later another shot was fired, and the President of the United States was dead.

In confusion bordering on panic, the President's car sped away and headed for Parkland Memorial Hospital, where the President was officially pronounced dead at 1:00 P.M. (CST).

Nine minutes after the first shot was fired, the CBS television network interrupted their programming with a bulletin: IN DALLAS THREE SHOTS WERE FIRED AT PRESIDENT KENNEDY'S MOTORCADE IN DOWNTOWN DALLAS. THE FIRST REPORTS SAY THAT THE PRESIDENT HAS BEEN SERIOUSLY WOUNDED BY THIS SHOOTING.

Less than an hour later, CBS again interrupted their programming: FROM DALLAS, TEXAS, THIS FLASH, APPARENTLY OFFICIAL, PRESIDENT KENNEDY DIED AT 1:00 P.M. (CST).

Only minutes after the shooting occurred, television had connected people to this incredible national tragedy. For the next three days, Americans across the country sat stunned before their television sets as they followed the events in Dallas and Washington. All the networks canceled all commercials.

Offices, schools, and businesses closed. People made their way home. For the rest of their lives millions of Americans would remember exactly where they were and what they were doing when they first heard the news. They would also remember their reactions — disbelief, sadness, shock, shame, and disgust.

Vice President Lyndon Johnson and his wife, under heavy Secret Service guard, were taken to Love Field outside Dallas, where they boarded the President's plane, *Air Force One*. After the President's body, accompanied by his wife, who never left his side, was placed aboard the plane, Johnson was sworn in as the thirty-sixth President of the United States. At 2:45 P.M. (CST) *Air Force One* departed Dallas for the capital.

Cabinet members and other high-ranking government officials hurriedly returned to Washington. Ted Kennedy, now a Senator from Massachusetts, flew to Hyannis Port to break the news to his father, who was still recovering from the stroke he had suffered two years earlier. After the death of two of their children, Rose felt they had already accepted a heavy load. Now Jack. It seemed almost unbelievable.

Early Friday evening, Robert Kennedy met his sister-in-law at Andrews Air Force base in Maryland, where *Air Force One* landed. Mrs. Kennedy carried herself with the composure and dignity that she would exhibit throughout the next three days.

Saturday morning a Mass was held for the President's family and friends in the East Room of the White House. Later that afternoon, President Johnson proclaimed Monday a national day of mourning. Few people thought that the next day, Sunday, would bring events that were almost as shocking as the assassination itself.

On his way out of the Texas Book Depository Building on Friday, Lee Harvey Oswald was stopped by a policeman. He was allowed to go after identifying himself as an employee of the Book Depository. He returned briefly to his rooming house, and when he was stopped once again by another policeman, he fired a pistol, killing the policeman. Oswald was captured at 1:50 P.M. (CST) in a movie theatre.

The situation in Dallas was tense and disorganized. The Dallas police presented the small, slight Oswald to the country at a news conference. In the basement of the Dallas jail late Friday night, Oswald said, "I really don't know what the situation is about. No one has told me anything. I do request someone to come forward and give me legal assistance."

Oswald was visited Saturday by his brother, mother, and Russian-born wife, Marina. People came and went all day and night in the Dallas jail. People who belonged there and people who didn't.

At 12:20 P.M. on Sunday, Oswald was led out of the jail elevator, through the basement and into the underground garage. Millions of television viewers inched forward in their chairs and on

Lee Harvey Oswald, President Kennedy's alleged assassin, being presented to newsmen in the Dallas police station.

their couches to get a close look at the man who was accused of killing the President. They saw Oswald handcuffed to a plainclothes Dallas policeman in a big, white Texas hat. The policeman led Oswald along while reporters crowded forward, moving in on Oswald and blocking the cameras. It was only later, in slow motion, that people would see the burly man — identified later as Jack Ruby — shoulder his way through the crowd. Ruby shot Oswald at point-blank range, killing him.

In the coming months, the question of who killed President Kennedy would become a national debate. Was Lee Harvey Oswald working with others? How many shots were there? From what direction did they come? Who fired them? With Oswald dead there was no trial, and the debate continues to this day.

Sunday afternoon was Mrs. Kennedy's first public appearance since the assassination. The President was lying in state in the East Room of the White House. When she appeared outside, holding the hands of her two children, the tragedy became sadly real and personal. The nation would long remember the procession of images, one sadder than the next, as the funeral procession on Monday took President Kennedy to Arlington National Cemetery, where he was buried.

Mrs. Kennedy, Caroline, John-John, Jack's brother Robert and sister Jean at the White House before joining the funeral procession.

President John F. Kennedy's body is taken to Arlington
National Cemetery. The riderless horse follows with boots
turned backward, symbolizing that the fallen leader will ride no
more.

Senator Patrick Moynihan, who was then assistant secretary of labor, was with journalist Mary McGrory. With tears in her eyes, Ms. McGrory said, "We'll never laugh again."

"Oh, we'll laugh again," Senator Moynihan responded. " . . . But we'll never be young again."

John F. Kennedy did not live long enough to fulfill the promise of his presidency. And the youthful spirit that moved so many Americans to attempt so much, never again burned so brightly.